When The Sky Meets The Sea

Spiritual Journey of Hope and Encouragement Through Inspirational Writings

Author

Nelida Montalvo

Illustrator

Emma Montalvo

Dedicated to the most Holy Trinity, the Blessed Virgin Mary, my parents, Julio and Neddie, and everyone who feels that they are not worthy of love... you are more than worthy because God said so... PERIOD.

Underneath Our Weakness There's Strength

Conversations with God

Inspirations

Underneath Our Weakness There's Strength

Don't Let Your Salt Lose its Flavor

Jesus said we are the salt of the earth

Called to bring out the best of one another
Enhance the goodness in each other
And purify wounds waiting to be healed

To cleanse injustice
Preserve our innocence
Season the heart to draw out love

Salt comes in many colors
Spread across the world
With a purpose that is endless

Don't let your salt lose its flavor
And the strength that it possesses
Salt is rock solid
And rock solid in love, is how God, made us to be

Human Frailty

I can't do this alone God
Writings words to uplift the hearts
When my heart is numb

To bring light
To those with only a flicker
When my light is barely lit

To provide comfort
For those who need consolation
When I'm in need of the same

I'm not apt for this
And I'm tired of trying

Why am I always left
To drink the bitter pill
And get over my pain

Why is it left on me
To bring happiness to those
Who don't even try

Humble myself
To apologize for issues
That others also contributed

Only to find that
No one feels the need
To do the same

As much as I want
To follow your ways
My humanity is beaten down

As much as I want
To turn the other cheek
There's nothing left on the other side

A New Dawn

Running in the meadow
The breeze softly
Caress her face

Arms flailing wildly
Laughing abandonly
With a freedom fresh as rain

Overwhelmed with joy
That cannot be contained
Touched by a light, hard to explain

With each new step
Vices deterred
And a brand-new manner, that emerge

Falling to the ground
Without a care
She rises up and leaps into air

Running faster
Desperate to fly
To see the soul with fresh eyes

It's dancing, it's singing
With this new dawn
Pure and clear like an angelic song

She rejoices and praise
Without cease
Because she knows He made her believe

The wonders of life
And what they can mean
For someone low, but now see

The talents within
Was taking its slumber
Awaken by light like rolling thunder

"How can this be?"
She only looked up
And blessings poured which couldn't be stopped

Just a glance
Is all He needs
For Him to say, "come with me"

As a glance is enough
For the graces to rain
For all He wants is to stop the pain

"My Love abounds
There's no limit
I have room for all, and those who reject it"

She flings into His arms
With all her might
Grateful for the mercy he gave her life

She couldn't let go, He didn't mind
He whispered softly...
"You were here the whole time"

The Bitter Taste of Forgiveness

For the prideful
Forgiveness is a medicine that is hard to swallow
Sour to the taste
Bitter to the tongue

It is a medicine that burns
Slowly moving down the throat
Like scalding honey
And bitter tea

Nausea is its side effect
A choking reflex
Sensation to heave
A need to chunder

It's like snakes venom
That carries no antidote
Coursing through the body
Leaving every limb...
numb

I'm Enough

There's a hole in my heart that I can't mend
Desperate for someone for the bleeding to end

Someone who'd take an interest in me
To make up for love not given to me

My heart will store the words that hurt
For an ounce of love to raise self-worth

I want to matter in someone's life
I'll be the dutiful, unassuming, unchallenging wife

All I need is for someone to want me
And I'll do anything even if it hurts me

But I fell harder than anyone could imagine
Deep into a pit surviving with rations

Up I peered and no one was there
Not even the person I thought would care

I called out for someone that would respond
But the voices just laughed and moved on

There I was alone in my thoughts
Coming to the realization that I was lost

Filled with despair because no one cared
Only worthy, if I had something to share

Menial, barren, full of sores
Worth less than a penny on the floor

My hands to my face
I'm just a mistake

My head cast down
Resigned and bound

Left alone to face the truth
My life tattered and of no use

Then something serene echoed above
It was a coo, a song, from a melodic dove

I felt a whisper and a gentle touch
Lovingly saying that I am enough

I quickly turned and gazed up
The voice said, "My children rise up"

I am perfect in God's eyes
An insult to Him, to believe otherwise

He slowly began to make me see
The wonderful person that is in me

He gave me talents to do many things
And don't need acceptance for me to sing

To Love myself without apologies
My faults, my flaws, and all my oddities

So if no one can accept the person in me
Inside, outside and in between

I will take the treasures that I want to give
And happily move on and continue to live

I am enough
The way I am
We're His masterpieces.... just as He planned

17

The Mountain's Peak Keeps Escaping Me

The mountain's peak keeps escaping me
The more I climb the farther it is
It's like a journey with no end in sight

Each climb full of uncertainty and fear
Pebbles crumble down, reminder that I can fall
Ascending, struggling against the pull of gravity

The mountain becomes narrow and rigid as I move forward
Each step becomes harder than the next
And as my breathing becomes staggered, hope seems to fade

The elusiveness of the mountains' peak is intentional
Guarding its' crest with passion
It blankets itself with snow and hides between the clouds

He tests my intentions
Questions the real purpose of the climb
Is it a selfless journey or for selfish glory?

To reach its pinnacle
Consistent loyalty to one's honorable purpose is essential
One must be ready to accept the responsibility of this achievement

The peak is very narrow
The difficulty in holding on is immense
Consistent faith and humility will keep you there

I continue the climb with struggle in tow
Hoping that every step rings true to its real purpose
Aware at every moment, ego and conceit will pull me down

And then the mountain's peak will keep escaping me

Persevere

Truth is at war with lies
Acceptance is battling denial
Trust confronts deceit
And Perseverance is a word that burns

Honor disrupts corruption
Peace confronts anger
Humility overwhelms pride
And Perseverance is a word that burns

Hope fights despair
Faith struggles unbelief
Love suffocates hate
And Perseverance is a word that burns

Conversations with God

Anger's Battle

There's a darkness that crawls within
Seeping through veins
Coursing through limbs

Fury of ten thousand waves
Crashing against the shore
Anger's rampage and furor to abhor

The strength of invincibility
Masked with pain
Mistaken for strength when it's rage

Its mission now is to consume the soul
To find the source
And destroy the core

Finding its way
Through its muddy trails
Feeling elated and yet with despair

Looking for something
Bright and serene
Onward it goes to destroy its gleam

The endless travails
Through rocky roads
Leading to places it will erode

At the corner of lies
Amidst valleys of corruption
Straight to the cave of total disruption

Where faith is entombed
And hope is not seen
Right in the street of lost dreams

But deep in the sunset
At a distance a sight
An island of love and wondrous might

Landed to destroy
The Holy contrary of ires
The divine, supreme, blessed fire

The Spirit is there
Tall and bright
Ready to protect the soul's life

Denying entry
Of that black shadow
That will raise its bow and shoot its arrow

The armor of goodness
Will not go down
And the shield of truth will stand its ground

"Dare if you may
To cross the line
The sword of love will slay the malign"

"Fear and hate
Is what you are
Trying to consume those near and far"

"You can fight
And you can persist
The soul will have my strength to resist"

"I am the light
That forever shines
And it will embrace all who are mine"

"Life is precious
This I'll save
With every breath till the end of days"

I Know

For the one who's lonely, I know
For the one who's scared, I know
For the one in despair, I know

My lonely child, hold my hand, I was lonely too
My fearful child, cling to me, as fear engulfed me too
My desperate child, trust me, my grace will pull you through

The Story of the Rag Doll

My rag doll
Beautiful and pure
Delicately stitched
And meticulously sewn

From a lovely shop
To which she was cared
Until the day she left
To find her trail

Her eyes open wide
She is awe-inspired
From the world she sees
And what her heart desires

She walks in joy
Through the trail she chose
Paved with flowers
Planted perfectly in rows

There was no guide
For my rag doll to follow
She wasn't aware
Of her trail of sorrow

As she walks ahead
She steps on a pebble
It makes a hole
Now her steps are unleveled

With a smile she continues
Even humming a song
She trips on a branch
And now a tear in her arm

My rag doll smirks
But decides to move on
Now she's anxious
Because things are going wrong

A crossroad appears
And she is perplexed
"Should I go to the right
Or to the left?"

Scared and uncertain
Her mind is hollow
Don't know where to go
With no guide to follow

To the right it is decided
The trail she chose
But the flowers aren't paved
Perfectly in rows

Sad and confused
But most of all tired
She sees a steep hill
That may lead to her desire

She makes the steep climb
Hoping her heart won't be shattered
A gust of wind pushes her down
Her legs and dress are tattered

Blinded with frustration
She turns back to the left trail
Where the flowers are wilted
And a musty scent invades the air

She is completely frayed
And hobbles through a broken fence
Certain she found her desire
But found that nothing made sense

A barn was on its side
Cows and ducks waving hi
Butterflies living in bee hives
And trees floating in the sky

The poor little rag doll
Angry and distraught
Angrily she cries,
"Where do I walk?!"

The sky opens up
And she sees the lovely shop
Where she was delicately stitched
And meticulously sewn up

A voice booms
From every part of the sky
It startles the rag doll
And searches for a tree to hide

"Listen here my little one
Come out from behind the tree
Please pay full attention
Because my Words will set you free"

"You have joyfully went on your journey
And have walked every trail
But there have been many cries
Because all your efforts fail"

"Why travel the trail on your own
As if you don't have a guide to follow
Please know that I'm always with you
Yesterday, today and tomorrow"

"You think that by leaving my shop
You are all alone
My shop is everywhere
Even under the smallest stone"

"You can pass me by
You can ignore me
But call my name
And you will find me"

"Look to me as your guide
To find your heart's desire
But know that at times
Some can't take you higher"

"I made you to prosper
Never to settle
Your dreams may be wonderful
But I can make them better"

"Understand that the things you seek
Can never be compared
To the abundant life
I have lovingly prepared"

"Trust in me
You will not go astray
I am the wisdom, the truth
And the way"

"Come to me
when you are tired
Come to me
When you feel alone"

"And believe me when I say
I live in the pocket of your little heart
That can never be tattered, frayed
And most of all, torn apart"

The Responsibility of Tending Flowers

I want to be like the birds
Pollinating the Rose, the Daffodils, the Lilies
The Irises, the Marigolds, and the Daisies

I want to fly high
Dropping seeds into every soil
For buds to come alive and happily uncoil

I want to be the rain
To reprieve their cries
While helping them sprout and come alive

I want to be the sun
Beaming rays to light and inspire
For the flowers to grow as tall as they aspire

How I wish to build a garden
Stretched for miles on end
With streams of flowers reaching out to Him

I have always wanted
To spread seeds, light, and water
For everyone to know the loving Father

He wants me to take this path
Full of objections I move along
With love he says,
"Embrace my gift and sing my song"

I'm paralyzed with fear
And want to believe He's wrong
He proudly declares,
"You came from me, so that makes you strong"

"You're not alone in this endeavor
My children possess this power
To bring out hope
and fragrance to the flower"

"Have trust in my Word
Live it at every blessed hour
To spark in hearts
the curiosity of my Fire"

"So move forward, for I am always here
And make those petals bloom with many colors
For I have given you the responsibility
of tending flowers"

Inspirations

The Master Painter

From His core, new life arises
Full of color made by the Master creator
Whose inspired painting, masterpieces cannot emulate

He starts by weaving a canvas delicately
Perfectly woven with the finest linen
Not one strand suffering imperfection

Once He's satisfied, He works on the base
The foundation that will support his painting
Allowing the work to take center stage

This stand is the cornerstone
The spine that will keep the painting erect
The back that will lovingly carry the weight

Ready to bring his work to life
The Master Painter creates different shapes
A singular form will not make the art sing

He wants a symphony of shapes
Like notes in a music sheet
All together creating a symphonic masterpiece

Enamored by the results
He moves forward with color
Combining shades to make the perfect palate

He cannot select one shade; He loves them all
Not one is better than the other
All must be added for the piece to be radiant

Every color works flawlessly together
And when those shades are mixed
An exquisite one emerges

But something is missing
And stares at the painting for a long while
Analyzing every piece of his work

He wonders if there are too many shapes
Are the colors not vibrant enough?
Why isn't this piece singing to him?

He puts aside the unfinished painting
And thinks about the message he wants to convey
What is the paintings' purpose and mission?

This goes on for a long time
He struggles to figure out the puzzle
A puzzle where all the pieces are scattered

And then he realizes
Each puzzle piece depends on each other
It needs one another to bring the image to life

The painter quickly finds his unfinished painting
He takes another look with fresh eyes
And smiles

He bands all of the colored shapes together
Intertwined to keep from breaking
Linked to create an intricate chain

He steps back to inspect His work
His heart full of emotion
Gives a tearful laugh

He finally found what the painting needed
What tied it together
What made it complete

It was simply,
Unity

The Garden

God knew what he was doing when he created nature. It's not just part of the world, it's medicine for the mind, body, soul, and spirit. It doesn't speak but yet it says so much.

One of my favorite places to visit is my church garden. I love how it fills me with serenity. It's a place that takes me away from the world. It centers me.

For a garden that is small, its humble surroundings overwhelm you with beauty that can take anyone's breath away. Emerald greenery, cascading bushes, pillowy grass, and majestic trees hunched inward seemingly protecting and embracing the garden and its inhabitants. The rays give the garden a simple yet fantastical scenery as it peeks through the trees searching for dews to make it sparkle like diamonds. But what ties this scenery together is the black solitary bench. It is where I pray my rosary while enjoying the peaceful sound of the breeze, the rustle of leaves, and the flower's sweet aroma as if imitating a mother's lullaby as she cradles her baby to sleep.

This little piece of earth is what keeps me sane when my world seems to be falling apart. It brings me back down to what truly matters in life... love. To love the fact that I made it to another day that I can spend with my daughter. Another chance to work on being a better person. Another day where I can make a person smile. An opportunity where I can give a piece of my love to someone who needs it.

In this world full of doing, the whole notion of slowing down and becoming aware of your surroundings goes out of mind. We forget what a wonderful world God has created for us. And instead of enjoying it we either destroy or ignore it. We refuse to stay still and observe the wonder. In the case of the garden, it is not concerned with being something else, there's no pretentions, there's no urgency. It accepts what it is, takes its time to grow, and is peaceful no matter what the seasons bring. It is just a garden that shares its joy to others because it can.

God knew what he was doing when he created nature. There are so many lessons we can learn. I believe that just like God dwells in us, he also dwells in all of Mother Nature. It is always seeking our attention both in subtle and not so subtle ways. From the leaves turning colors, trees providing shade, overgrown bushes, the boom of thunder, the sound of rain... it is desperate for our attention. And if you think about it, aren't we the same in our own way? Every living thing and being has a voice and we all should give those voices a chance to speak and to be heard. A chance to share their beauty. But the only way we can experience the beauty, is if we stay still, listen, and observe the wonder.

Use Your Light

Use your light

Be the sunlight the moon depends
The sunrise to every darkness
The beam that breaks the clouds
The rainbow after the rain
The rays that make life grow

Be the brilliance to aspire
The soldier of illumination
The enlightenment to anger
The firelight for warmth
The lamp without its shade

And if by chance
Your light begins to dim
Like a candle losing its wick
Turn to the One whose light is eternal
And shines with a radiance of ten million suns

His beacon is never far
Just follow the blaze of love
That leads to his home
His star
Burning brightly
in your heart

Vainglory Temptation

Temptation should be called agony
Its blade never dulls
It is sharpened with each cut

The searing pain
Working through your mind
Each time the knife strikes

Manipulating whispers with its whip
Lashing until gashes form
Then salted with stinging guilt

It plays with your desires when resistance attacks
Side blinds you with instigation
Uses past hurts that were never healed

It repeatedly beats you down
To the point you don't know yourself
And you finally succumb to its hold

This prolific playwright
And its vainglory stories
Demands a stellar performance

I cannot fathom what Jesus felt
While in agony in the garden
As temptation played its game

The weight on His shoulders
Heavier than any of us could ever carry
Brought Him down to His knees

But He beat this disease
He showed us it was possible
Through Him we will find the cure

So the next time temptation demands a performance...

Turn to the True Prolific Playwright
Where vainglory is transformed into sacrificial love
Whose life inspires
And His stories teach truth

Because when you know the truth
Temptation has no choice but to sit back
And see our OWN stellar performance

Up on the Blessed Tree

Jesus was always seeking those in need
Always forging ahead planting seeds

He shouldered crosses that made him weary
Helping those who alone can't carry

Breaking down the wall of fear
So all can live a life with zeal

Building bridges so many can cross
So no one feels they are lost

The trials and battles often waged
But he kept on moving turning each page

Why did he care about others' plight?
Because our battle is his fight

He fought his way to correct our wrong
Because his works will never be gone

From cities to towns, he never stopped
Preaching what is good and what is not

He never tired and performed his signs
Because he knew he was on borrowed time

There was one last thing he needed to do
That would complete his mission and all would be good

Moving forward he started to pray
"Help me have this ransom paid"

Finally, he reached the intended place
Where his final mission would be faced

There it was, a blessed tree
Anxiously waiting for its leaves

He laid on it and said, "it will be done"
And that's when they both meld into one

He caught his weeping mother, at first sight
And said to her "Mama, I will be alright"

Then all was silent, not a word said
You could hear life, in the ocean bed

Everything, frozen in time
As if minutes and hours was standing by

He suddenly lifts his head to speak
He yells, "my God their soul to keep"!
"Please forgive their unbelief
For they do not know what they reap"

He held on to his final breath
Enough, to complete His test

And then with a smile, wider than the sea
He looked up and proudly said,
"Father, they are free"

Nature Honors Our Blessed Mother

What a glorious day God has made
Nature honors
Our Blessed Mother
Each day

Blue skies and pillowy clouds
Emulate an embrace
Our Blessed Mother
Gifts in her blue and white gown

Undulating oceans and calming seas
Which mimics
Our Blessed Mother
As she cradles us to dream

The gentle breeze sways the trees
Motioning the way
Our Blessed Mother
Comforts all who needs

Rain stream down our faces
In imitation
Our Blessed Mother
Showering graces

The sun beams the morning rays
Like a morning kiss
Our Blessed Mother
Gives each day

May the Lord Keep you Safe in His Arms

May the Lord keep you safe in His arms

As he refreshes like an inspiring song

Providing the anchor of faith to keep you strong

Because the Lord's promise is never wrong

He will be there from dusk to dawn

Ensuring that suffering does not dim His song

The Sky Meets the Sea

Look to the horizon
From the sea to the sky
And imagine how much love, one can find

Yes, the distance is extreme
And may be hard to see
But as you look farther away
The sky meets the sea

It's all interconnected
Invisible to the eye
Love is everywhere, easy to find

No need to know where it began
Doesn't matter where it starts
Just have faith, it will find many hearts

Sing as loud as you can
Your song will take flight
The wind will carry it to new heights

Don't ever believe your message is lost
It is traveling to many parts
Busy reviving ailing hearts

So never fear that your song has died
It's searching for a brand-new sunrise
Cradled right between the sea and the sky

And yes, the distance is extreme
With no connection in between
But remember to look farther away
And you'll see that the sky will meet the sea

Acknowledgements:

This could not have been possible if it wasn't for the love and guidance of the all mighty Lord. Before I would begin my writings, I would pray to the Holy Spirit to provide me with the words... and he delivered. Phrases would pop up in my head that I would never in a million years would have come up by myself. I always wanted to counsel others and provide encouragement and I am thankful that God gave me the vehicle to do so in writing. I'm not the best writer in the world, but to me, words are powerful. It can break or uplift a heart and although my writing style is raw, it comes entirely from the heart.

Speaking of writing, I must mention my hero, O. Henry (William Sydney Porter) – the one that started it all. When I was a little girl, I was not an avid reader because I had issues with comprehension and speech but that all changed when I was introduced to The Last Leaf at grammar school; that beautiful story changed everything. It propelled me to become a certified bookworm with the audacity to produce writings despite my issues with comprehension and communication.

I also want to thank my strong and amazing parents, Julio and Neddie for not only teaching myself and my brothers morality, responsibility, and integrity but inculcating the importance of having a relationship with God. I wouldn't know where my life would be if I didn't have the beautiful bond that I have with the Lord today.

My brothers Julio, Rolando, and my sister-in-law, Diana, who are always there whenever I need a hug and encouragement. My cousins Erica and Lilliana who gave me their shoulder when I was going through a dark time in my life. Emma, my beautiful niece who created the cover for this book; her talent is astounding at such a young age and it will only get better - Titi loves you more than you can ever imagine. To Patricia and Elmer, my daughter's paternal grandparents. Thank you so very much for your encouragement and being dedicated grandparents to my daughter. Words cannot express how grateful I am. My entire family whom I adore with all my heart and soul – I thank God I was placed to be part of this crazy, fun loving group.

A big thank you to the St. Anne's bible class in Fairlawn, NJ where I first started my journey in learning more about the Word of God; I got addicted. Father Colin, who lifted me up when I couldn't do it myself; you helped me see my worth. Josefina, who is much more than my therapist, she is a great friend; you have helped me sort out and make sense the fractured pieces of my mind, I will always be grateful. My best friend (really sister) since high-school (30 years) Luz who has always been by my side cheering me on. To my wonderful friends, Yisell, Lisa, Linda, and Gerard for taking the time to study the bible together. I learned so much from you, your wisdom and faith in the Lord is grand and inspirational. Elle, Kelly and Yesenia for always being supportive and lifting me up whenever I needed a dose of inspiration.

To the love of my entire life, my daughter Cassandra, who inspires me every single day with her intelligence, wit, humor, and kind soul. She is my world; I am humbled and thankful that God teamed myself and her father, Nolan, the privilege to raise this wonderful human being. We are so proud of her. And finally, I thank YOU, the reader, for giving me the opportunity to share my writings with you. My goal is to simply uplift hearts and show that you are unconditionally loved... always.

About the Author

Nelida is an aspiring author who enjoys writing poetry and stories pertaining life's adventures and how the Lord is always right beside us throughout those adventures. Her goal in her writings is to simply encourage and remind all who are willing to listen that Jesus is here yesterday, today, tomorrow, and to infinity. He will always be by our side in our good moments and lovingly comfort and guide us through our not so good moments. He's just waiting for your door to open and invite him in.

For more of Nelida's work you can visit her blog page called "Reflection Sparks" at www.reflectionsparks.com[1] where she writes about life's reflections regarding struggles and successes and what she has learned from them using God's teachings.

We love because he first loved us – 1 John 4:19 (NIV)

---

1. http://www.reflectionsparks.com